Aunt Phil's Trunk

Student Workbook

for

The Call of the Wild

and

Other Northland Stories

BY
JACK LONDON

Jack London's Journey to Fame and Fortune
By Laurel Downing Bill

Front Cover Art by Kim Sherry

Student Workbook

for

The Call of the Wild

and

Other Northland Stories

STORIES BY
JACK LONDON

CURRICULUM BY
LAUREL DOWNING BILL

Special thanks to Nicole Cruz for her assitance in makng this student workbook and its accompanying teacher guide for *The Call of the Wild and Other Northland Stories*

Aunt Phil's Trunk LLC, Anchorage, Alaska
www.auntphilstrunk.com
Copyright © 2017 by Laurel Downing Bill
Reprinted 2023

All rights reserved. No part of this book may be used or reproduced in any manner whatsoever without written permission from the author, except in the case of brief quotations embodied in critical articles and reviews

ISBN: 978-1-940479-16-3

Welcome to *The Call of the Wild* and Other Northland Stories Curriculum

The Call of the Wild and Other Northland Stories curriculum is designed to be used as part of a ninth- or tenth-grade language arts curriculum.

You will begin by reading and analyzing one of Jack London's classic novels, *The Call of the Wild*. Reading one chapter at a time, you will learn new vocabulary words and answer comprehension and discussion questions for each chapter. You also will explore the meaning of key quotes from the chapter and analyze the main theme of the reading. Each lesson concludes with a writing exercise to encourage deeper interaction with the text, as well as practice creative writing skills.

In the second section of the curriculum, you will read several of Jack London's short stories. Each lesson includes vocabulary words, discussion questions, key quotes from the story, and an opportunity to write a short summary of the story. The writing exercises in this unit encourage creative writing and some imitation of techniques used by London.

The curriculum concludes with a lesson on the life of Jack London. You will begin by reading several short chapters to learn about his life. Next, you will answer comprehension and discussion questions about the reading. The lesson concludes with a final essay on one of three options.

I hope that you enjoy this journey into the life and stories of one of America's most beloved authors, Jack London.

NOTE: Racial slurs in *A Thousand Deaths* by Jack London

Sometimes Jack London uses racial slurs in his writing. Especially in the final short story you will read in this curriculum titled, *A Thousand Deaths*. The presence of words of this type in this curriculum in no way condones the use of them. We wanted this story included in this collection because it is the story that basically launched London's career as a writer in 1899.

While compiling this collection of stories, we considered changing some words to reflect how attitudes have changed since London wrote his works. But we felt it more important to keep his writings in tact as he first wrote them.

You may want to think about why London may have used such terms in 1899, and why it is not typical to see these terms in modern literature. Most importantly, consider why these words are hurtful and unacceptable for anyone to use in any context. After all …

"Those who cannot remember the past are condemned to repeat it."
– George Santayana

Jack London (b. Jan. 12, 1876 – d. Nov. 22, 1916) was a prolific fiction writer. Many people got their first glimpse of life in the northland by reading his stories of the Klondike.

TABLE OF CONTENTS

The Call of the Wild
Lesson 1 – Into the Primitive	6
Lesson 2 – The Law of Club and Fang	12
Lesson 3 – The Dominant Primordial	18
Lesson 4 – Who Has Won to Mastership	24
Lesson 5 – The Toil of Trace and Trail	30
Lesson 6 – For the Love of a Man	36
Lesson 7 – The Sounding of the Call	42
Wild Vocabulary Crossword Puzzle	48

Other Northland Stories
To the Man on the Trail	50
The White Silence	56
The Son of the Wolf	62
The Men of Forty Mile	68
In a Far Country	74
The Priestly Prerogative	80
The Wife of the King	86
The Wisdom of the Trail	92
An Odyssey of the North	98
To Build a Fire	104

Jack London's Journey
Toward Fame and Fortune/In His Own Words	110
Final Essay	113
Northland Vocabulary Crossword Puzzle	118
Extra paper for lessons	120

THE CALL OF THE WILD

LESSON 1: INTO THE PRIMITIVE

BEFORE YOU READ

Quote from the Reading

Look for this quote in your reading and pay special attention to its context:

"London's message that civilization is a thin veneer that can, under certain circumstances, disappear and return one to a wild state is as relevant today as it was when he wrote this story more than 100 years ago." – From the introduction

VOCABULARY

Look for these words in your reading:

Primitive – belonging to or characteristic of an early stage of development
Demesne – domain; land actually possessed by the lord of an estate and not held by tenants
Insular – protected; inexperienced
Calamity – an event that causes great harm; deep distress or misery
Dormant – not active but capable of becoming active

READING

Read: Introduction, Cast of Characters and Chapter 1 in your textbook (Pages 5-17)

NOW THAT YOU'VE READ THE ASSIGNED CHAPTER

After reading Chapter 1, what do you think the author meant by the quote above?

_____
_____
_____
_____
_____
_____
_____
_____
_____
_____
_____
_____

COMPREHENSION

1) Where does the beginning of the story take place? Why did Jack London choose this setting to open his book? Buck lived in California. It would be easier to transport Buck from California to Alaska because they are coastal.

2) Who is the main character of the book? What do we learn about this character in Chapter 1? A dog named Buck. He lived a good life in California.

3) Who was Manuel? Why did he steal Buck? Manuel is a gardener. He stole Buck because he heard of gold and had gambling addictions.

4) How does the man with the red sweater treat Buck? Why? The man treated buck terribly with a club. He was forcing Buck to be submissive.

DISCUSSION

What is the significance of the title of Chapter 1? Buck was leaving civilization.

WRITING EXERCISE

As you read in the introduction, Jack London based *The Call of the Wild* on places and people that he met in his life. The main character, Buck, closely resembled a dog that the Bond family loaned to the author while he was in the Klondike. Great fiction often comes from our life experiences. Write a one-page short story that is inspired by a place or an event that is special to you. Try to convey your feelings about the place or the event in your writing.

LESSON ONE: INTO THE PRIMITIVE

Comprehension Questions _____ (10 pts. per question – possible 40 pts.)
Discussion Question _____ (possible 10 pts.)

Writing Exercise
    Originality and Creativity _____ (possible 10 pts.)
    Overall Organization _____ (possible 10 pts.)
    Language and Style _____ (possible 10 pts.)
    Composition is neat _____ (possible 10 pts.)
    Grammar and Spelling _____ (possible 10 pts.)

                                            Total _____

THE CALL OF THE WILD

LESSON 2: THE LAW OF CLUB AND FANG

BEFORE YOU READ

Quote from the Reading

Look for this quote in your reading and pay special attention to its context:

"He had been suddenly jerked from the heart of civilization and flung into the heart of things primordial."

VOCABULARY

Look for these words in your reading:

Diabolically – with evil intent
Primordial – first created or developed
Dignity – quality or state of being worthy or esteemed
Disconsolate – very sad
Antagonist – one who contends with or opposes another

READING

Read: Chapter 2 (Pages 18-26)

NOW THAT YOU'VE READ THE ASSIGNED CHAPTER

Who was the quote above about? Rewrite it in your own words.

_____
_____
_____
_____
_____
_____
_____
_____
_____
_____
_____
_____
_____
_____

COMPREHENSION

1) What tragedy occurred on Buck's first day in the Yukon? What did he learn from it?

_____
_____
_____
_____

2) What dogs did Buck meet in Chapter 2? Describe them. _____

_____
_____
_____
_____
_____

3) What was the law of club and fang? How was this different from the laws that Buck previously lived by on Judge Miller's ranch? _____

_____
_____
_____
_____

4) Describe how Buck learns to become a sled dog. _____

_____
_____
_____
_____

DISCUSSION

Jack London tells the story from the point of view of the main character, Buck. How do you think this story would be different if it was told from the point of view of a human character?

_____
_____
_____
_____
_____
_____
_____

WRITING EXERCISE

The term "point of view" originates from the Latin phrase, punctum visus, which means "position from which a thing is viewed." By using the point of view of an animal, Jack London gives a unique interpretation of the events that occur in this fictional tale. Choose one of your favorite stories and rewrite a scene from it using the point of view of an animal.

LESSON TWO: THE LAW OF CLUB AND FANG

Comprehension Questions _____ (10 pts. per question – possible 40 pts.)
Discussion Question _____ (possible 10 pts.)

Writing Exercise
    Originality and Creativity   _____ (possible 10 pts.)
    Overall Organization   _____ (possible 10 pts.)
    Language and Style   _____ (possible 10 pts.)
    Composition is neat   _____ (possible 10 pts.)
    Grammar and Spelling   _____ (possible 10 pts.)

        Total _____

THE CALL OF THE WILD
LESSON 3: THE DOMINANT PRIMORDIAL BEAST

BEFORE YOU READ

Quote from the Reading

Look for this quote in your reading and pay special attention to its context:

"The dark circle became a dot on the moon-flooded snow as Spitz disappeared from view. Buck stood and looked on, the successful champion, the dominant primordial beast who had made his kill and found it good."

VOCABULARY

Look for these words in your reading:

Marauders – one who roams about in search of things to steal
Covert – not openly made or done
Insidious – sinister; dangerous
Supremacy – supreme power or authority
Inexorable – unstoppable or relentless

READING

Read: Chapter 3 (Pages 27-39)

NOW THAT YOU'VE READ THE ASSIGNED CHAPTER

What do you think the author meant when he called Buck a "dominant primordial beast" in the quote above?

_____
_____
_____
_____
_____
_____
_____
_____
_____
_____
_____

COMPREHENSION

1) How do Buck and Spitz become rivals?

2) Describe the wild dogs that were searching for food at the camp. How were they different than any dog that Buck had ever seen?

3) In what ways do Francois and Perrault show compassion for the dogs in this chapter?

4) Describe the fight at the end of the chapter between Buck and Spitz.

DISCUSSION

Do you think that Buck's time on the Yukon prepared him for this fight with Spitz? Do you think that Buck would have won the fight if it had happened before he was kidnapped and taken to the Yukon? Explain your answers.

WRITING EXERCISE

Have you ever experienced a bully like Spitz? Write about a time that you or someone you know was bullied. Describe the bully and at least one interaction with the bully. How did the person being bullied respond? Conclude with your thoughts on the best way to handle being bullied.

LESSON THREE: THE DOMINANT PRIMORDIAL BEAST

Comprehension Questions _____ (10 pts. per question – possible 40 pts.)
Discussion Question _____ (possible 10 pts.)

Writing Exercise
    Originality and Creativity   _____ (possible 10 pts.)
    Overall Organization   _____ (possible 10 pts.)
    Language and Style   _____ (possible 10 pts.)
    Composition is neat   _____ (possible 10 pts.)
    Grammar and Spelling   _____ (possible 10 pts.)

                      Total _____

THE CALL OF THE WILD

LESSON 4: WHO HAS WON TO MASTERSHIP

BEFORE YOU READ

Quote from the Reading

Look for this quote in your reading and pay special attention to its context:

"But it was in giving the law and making his mates live up to it that Buck excelled."

VOCABULARY

Look for these words in your reading:

Manifested – clear to the senses
Obdurate – stubborn
Lugubriously – sadly
Perplexed – confused

READING

Read: Chapter 4 (Pages 40-47)

NOW THAT YOU'VE READ THE ASSIGNED CHAPTER

The quote above describes the kind of leader that Buck became in Chapter 4. How would you describe Buck as a leader?

_____
_____
_____
_____
_____
_____
_____
_____
_____
_____
_____
_____
_____
_____

COMPREHENSION

1) How did Francois and Perrault react when they discovered that Buck killed Spitz? Which dog did they choose to make lead dog? What did Buck do about this?

2) What happened when the team got to Skagway?

3) Describe the man that Buck "sees" by the fire. Who or what do you think this man symbolizes?

4) Why did the new owner shoot Dave at the end of the chapter?

DISCUSSION

If you could choose one word to describe Dave's death, what would it be? Why?

WRITING EXERCISE

Authors often use dreams to communicate or highlight an important theme in the story, just as Jack London used Buck's dream of a hairy, rugged man to symbolize a key theme in his story. Write a short fictional story that centers around a dream.

LESSON FOUR: WHO HAS WON TO MASTERSHIP

Comprehension Questions _____ (10 pts. per question – possible 40 pts.)
Discussion Question _____ (possible 10 pts.)

Writing Exercise
    Originality and Creativity   _____ (possible 10 pts.)
    Overall Organization   _____ (possible 10 pts.)
    Language and Style   _____ (possible 10 pts.)
    Composition is neat   _____ (possible 10 pts.)
    Grammar and Spelling   _____ (possible 10 pts.)

                                   Total _____

THE CALL OF THE WILD

LESSON 5: THE TOIL OF TRACE AND TRAIL

BEFORE YOU READ

Quote from the Reading

Look for this quote in your reading and pay special attention to its context:

"The wonderful patience of the trail that comes to men who toil hard and suffer sore, and remain sweet of speech and kindly, did not come to these two men and the woman."

VOCABULARY

Look for these words in your reading:

Salient – important
Jaded – dull; apathetic
Slovenly – untidy
Voracious – very powerful
Inarticulate – difficulty expressing with words

READING

Read: Chapter 5 (Pages 48-61)

NOW THAT YOU'VE READ THE ASSIGNED CHAPTER

Who is the quote above about? What do you think the author meant by this?

_____
_____
_____
_____
_____
_____
_____
_____
_____
_____
_____
_____
_____

COMPREHENSION

1) Describe Hal and Charles.

2) What did Buck think about his new owners?

3) What were some of the reasons that Hal, Charles and Mercedes were behind schedule?

4) Why did Buck refuse to lead the team?

DISCUSSION

Reread the opening four lines of Chapter 1. These lines are from a poem by John Meyers O'Hara called "Atavism" that Jack London thought reflected the theme of The Call of the Wild. Do you agree with him? Explain why or why not?

WRITING EXERCISE

How would you summarize the theme of *The Call of the Wild* for someone who hasn't read the book yet? Write a poem that reflects your thoughts.

LESSON FIVE: THE TOIL OF TRACE AND TRAIL

Comprehension Questions _____ (10 pts. per question – possible 40 pts.)
Discussion Question _____ (possible 10 pts.)

Writing Exercise
    Originality and Creativity   _____ (possible 10 pts.)
    Overall Organization   _____ (possible 10 pts.)
    Language and Style   _____ (possible 10 pts.)
    Composition is neat   _____ (possible 10 pts.)
    Grammar and Spelling   _____ (possible 10 pts.)

                            Total _____

THE CALL OF THE WILD

LESSON 6: FOR THE LOVE OF A MAN

BEFORE YOU READ

Quote from the Reading

Look for this quote in your reading and pay special attention to its context:

"He was older than the days he had seen and the breaths he had drawn."

VOCABULARY

Look for these words in your reading:

Eloquent – forceful or fluent expression
Reverently – very respectful
Transient – not lasting or staying too long
Tenderfoot – a beginner

READING

Read: Chapter 6 (Pages 62-74)

NOW THAT YOU'VE READ THE ASSIGNED CHAPTER

What do you think the author meant by the quote above?

_____
_____
_____
_____
_____
_____
_____
_____
_____
_____
_____
_____
_____
_____
_____
_____
_____

COMPREHENSION

1) Was Buck's relationship with John Thornton different than his relationship with his other owners? Explain your answer. _____
_____
_____
_____
_____

2) How did Buck show his affection for John Thornton? _____
_____
_____
_____
_____

3) Describe one of the two times that Buck saved John Thornton's life. _____
_____
_____
_____

4) What bet did John Thornton make? Did he win the bet? _____
_____
_____
_____
_____

DISCUSSION

What similarities do you see between Buck and John Thornton?
_____
_____
_____
_____
_____
_____
_____
_____
_____
_____

WRITING EXERCISE

Write a poem, song or letter from Buck to John Thornton explaining his call to the wild. Try to convey Buck's feelings of wanting to stay loyal to John, yet still needing to abide by the law of club and fang.

LESSON SIX: FOR THE LOVE OF A MAN

Comprehension Questions _____ (10 pts. per question – possible 40 pts.)
Discussion Question _____ (possible 10 pts.)

Writing Exercise
    Originality and Creativity   _____ (possible 10 pts.)
    Overall Organization   _____ (possible 10 pts.)
    Language and Style   _____ (possible 10 pts.)
    Composition is neat   _____ (possible 10 pts.)
    Grammar and Spelling   _____ (possible 10 pts.)

                      Total _____

THE CALL OF THE WILD

LESSON 7: THE SOUNDING OF THE CALL

BEFORE YOU READ

Quote from the Reading

Look for this quote in your reading and pay special attention to its context:

"He knew he was at last answering the call, running by the side of his wood brother toward the place from where the call surely came."

VOCABULARY

Look for these words in your reading:

Ramshackle – run-down
Formidable – causing fear or dread
Sequential – in order
Muses – to ponder or reflect
Discomfited – to put into a state of perplexity or embarrassment

READING

Read: Chapter 7 (Pages 75-89)

NOW THAT YOU'VE READ THE ASSIGNED CHAPTER

What do you think the author meant by the quote above?

_____
_____
_____
_____
_____
_____
_____
_____
_____
_____
_____
_____
_____
_____

COMPREHENSION

1) What adventure did Buck, John and his partners go on after John won the bet? Did Buck enjoy this adventure?

2) What happened when Buck met a timber wolf in the woods?

3) How did his love of John Thornton cause Buck to "lose his head"?

4) Jack London uses many events throughout the book to foreshadow the ending. Were you surprised by the ending? Were there any events that might have given you a clue to the ending?

DISCUSSION

After completing the novel, which characters would you call wild? Which characters would you call civilized? Explain why.

WRITING EXERCISE

The Call of the Wild is considered a great piece of literature. What do you consider to be three characteristics of a great novel? Write a persuasive letter to a friend who is not interested in reading *The Call of the Wild*. Explain why *The Call of the Wild* is a great novel using those three characteristics and supporting details from the novel.

LESSON SEVEN: THE SOUNDING OF THE CALL

Comprehension Questions _____ (10 pts. per question – possible 40 pts.)
Discussion Question _____ (possible 10 pts.)

Writing Exercise
    Originality and Creativity _____ (possible 10 pts.)
    Overall Organization _____ (possible 10 pts.)
    Language and Style _____ (possible 10 pts.)
    Composition is neat _____ (possible 10 pts.)
    Grammar and Spelling _____ (possible 10 pts.)

Total _____

Wild Vocabulary
Crossword Puzzle

Read the Across and Down clues and fill in the blank boxes that match the number on the clues

ACROSS

5 Forceful or fluent expression
6 First created or developed
9 Very powerful
13 With evil intent
16 Quality or state of being worthy or esteemed
19 One who contends with or opposes another
22 Not active but capable of becoming active
25 In order
26 Confused
27 Unstoppable or relentless
28 Stubborn
30 To ponder or reflect
31 An event that causes great harm; deep distress or misery
32 Belonging to or characteristic of an early stage of development
33 Untidy

DOWN

1 Not openly made or done
2 Supreme power or authority
3 Protected; inexperienced
4 Causing fear or dread
7 Difficulty expressing with words
8 To put into a state of perplexity or embarrassment
10 Very sad
11 Sinister; dangerous
12 Run-down
14 Sadly
15 Clear to the senses
17 Not lasting or staying too long
18 Domain; land actually possessed by the lord of an estate and not held by tenants
20 A beginner
21 One who roams about in search of things to steal
23 Important
24 Very respectful
29 Dull; apathetic

Wild Vocabulary
Crossword Puzzle

Read the Across and Down clues and fill in the blank boxes that match the number on the clues

NORTHLAND STORIES

LESSON 8: TO THE MAN ON THE TRAIL

BEFORE YOU READ

Quote from the Reading

Look for this quote in your reading and pay special attention to its context:

"It was evident that they were angry – first, at the way they had been deceived; and second, at the outraged ethics of the Northland, where honesty, above all, was man's prime jewel."

VOCABULARY

Look for these words in your reading:

Benignantly – showing kindly feelings or intentions
Pertinacity – stubbornly or annoyingly persistent
Monotonous – boring from being always the same

READING

Read: *To the Man on the Trail* (Pages 90-99)

NOW THAT YOU'VE READ THE ASSIGNED STORY

Reread the quote above. To whom is the author referring? Why are they angry?

STORY SUMMARY

Summarize *To the Man on the Trail* below. How would you describe the theme of this story? _____

DISCUSSION

After reading this short story and the *Call of the Wild*, how would you describe life for an adventurer in the Northland? What words come to mind?

WRITING EXERCISE

Write your own song or poem about life as an adventurer in the Northland. Use some of the words that you brainstormed in the discussion question. You will receive a bonus point for every vocabulary word you include.

LESSON EIGHT: TO THE MAN ON THE TRAIL

Story Summary _____ (possible 40 pts.)
Discussion Question _____ (possible 10 pts.)

Writing Exercise
    Originality and Creativity   _____ (possible 10 pts.)
    Overall Organization   _____ (possible 10 pts.)
    Language and Style   _____ (possible 10 pts.)
    Composition is neat   _____ (possible 10 pts.)
    Grammar and Spelling   _____ (possible 10 pts.)

                         Total _____

    Bonus Points for Vocabulary Words Used   _____

NORTHLAND STORIES

LESSON 9: THE WHITE SILENCE

BEFORE YOU READ

Quote from the Reading

Look for this quote in your reading and pay special attention to its context:

"Don't send her back to her people, Kid. It's beastly hard for a woman to go back."

VOCABULARY

Look for these words in your reading:

Ruefully – pity or sympathy
Propinquity – nearness in place or time
Primeval – relating to a primitive or early age

READING

Read: *The White Silence* (Pages 100-108)

NOW THAT YOU'VE READ THE ASSIGNED STORY

Reread the quote above. Who said this quote? What did he mean by this statement?

STORY SUMMARY

Summarize *White Silence* below. How would you describe the theme of this story?

DISCUSSION

Why do you think the author titled this story, "White Silence"?

WRITING EXERCISE

Write a short essay that answers these questions:
1) Are you beginning to see common themes among Jack London's writings? If so, what are they?
2) Can you think of another story written by a different author that shares a similar theme? Include specific examples from the stories to support your answer.

LESSON NINE: THE WHITE SILENCE

Story Summary _____ (possible 40 pts.)
Discussion Question _____ (possible 10 pts.)

Writing Exercise
    Originality and Creativity _____ (possible 10 pts.)
    Overall Organization _____ (possible 10 pts.)
    Language and Style _____ (possible 10 pts.)
    Composition is neat _____ (possible 10 pts.)
    Grammar and Spelling _____ (possible 10 pts.)

Total _____

NORTHLAND STORIES

LESSON 10: THE SON OF THE WOLF

BEFORE YOU READ

Quote from the Reading

Look for this quote in your reading and pay special attention to its context:

"If, in the days to come, thou shouldst journey to the Country of the Yukon, know thou that there shall always be a place and much food by the fire of the Wolf. The night is now passing into the day. I go, but I may come again. And for the last time, remember the Law of the Wolf!"

VOCABULARY

Look for these words in your reading:

Malady – a disease or disorder of the body or mind
Anomaly – something different, abnormal or strange
Anachronism – a person or a thing out of place in time

READING

Read: *The Son of the Wolf* (Pages 110-124)

NOW THAT YOU'VE READ THE ASSIGNED STORY

Reread the quote above. What was the "law of the wolf"?

_____
_____
_____
_____
_____
_____
_____
_____
_____
_____
_____
_____
_____

STORY SUMMARY

Summarize *The Son of the Wolf* below. How would you describe the theme of this story?

DISCUSSION

Why do you think the Tanana people called Mackenzie "Son of Wolf"?

WRITING EXERCISE

Compare and contrast the cultures of Mackenzie and Zarinska. Can you find any similarities between the two? How are they different? How do the differences impact both Mackenzie and Zarinksa? Write a short essay answering each of these questions.

LESSON TEN: THE SON OF THE WOLF

Story Summary _____ (possible 40 pts.)
Discussion Question _____ (possible 10 pts.)

Writing Exercise
    Originality and Creativity _____ (possible 10 pts.)
    Overall Organization _____ (possible 10 pts.)
    Language and Style _____ (possible 10 pts.)
    Composition is neat _____ (possible 10 pts.)
    Grammar and Spelling _____ (possible 10 pts.)

        Total _____

NORTHLAND STORIES

LESSON 11: THE MEN OF FORTY MILE

BEFORE YOU READ

Quote from the Reading

Look for this quote in your reading and pay special attention to its context:

"There was no law in the land. The mounted police was also a thing of the future. Each man measured an offense, and meted out the punishment inasmuch as it affected himself."

VOCABULARY

Look for these words in your reading:

Caste – a division of society based upon differences of wealth, rank, or occupation
Remonstrances – an act or instance of protest
Paradoxal – contradictory or opposed to common sense

READING

Read: *The Men of Forty Mile* (Pages 125-133)

NOW THAT YOU'VE READ THE ASSIGNED STORY

Reread the quote above. How do you think the story would be different if there were mounted police?

_____
_____
_____
_____
_____
_____
_____
_____
_____
_____
_____
_____
_____
_____
_____
_____

STORY SUMMARY

Summarize *The Men of Forty Mile* below.

DISCUSSION

Imagine that you are a friend of Bettles and Lon in the story. What would you do to try to stop them from fighting?

WRITING EXERCISE

Jack London often employs the use of different dialects in his stories to make his characters more authentic. Write your own short story that takes place anywhere in the world. Include at least one scene where the characters speak in a dialect that one might encounter in your chosen setting.

LESSON ELEVEN: THE MEN OF FORTY MILE

Story Summary _____ (possible 40 pts.)
Discussion Question _____ (possible 10 pts.)

Writing Exercise
    Originality and Creativity _____ (possible 10 pts.)
    Overall Organization _____ (possible 10 pts.)
    Language and Style _____ (possible 10 pts.)
    Composition is neat _____ (possible 10 pts.)
    Grammar and Spelling _____ (possible 10 pts.)

                        Total _____

NORTHLAND STORIES

LESSON 12: IN A FAR COUNTRY

BEFORE YOU READ

Quote from the Reading

Look for this quote in your reading and pay special attention to its context:

"When a man journeys into a far country, he must be prepared to forget many of the things he has learned, and to acquire such customs as are inherent with existence in the new land..."

VOCABULARY

Look for these words in your reading:

Adaptability – suited by nature, character or design to a particular use
Vicissitudes – a surprising or irregular change
Badinage – playful banter

READING

Read: *In a Far Country* (Pages 134-149)

NOW THAT YOU'VE READ THE ASSIGNED STORY

Reread the quote above. What "things" and "customs" is the author referring to in this quote?

_____
_____
_____
_____
_____
_____
_____
_____
_____
_____
_____
_____
_____
_____
_____
_____

STORY SUMMARY

Summarize *In a Far Country* below. Describe the main characters of the story.

DISCUSSION

As you read about Carter Weatherbee and Percy Cuthfert, did you think that the story would end badly for them? What were the clues in the story that led you to think that?

WRITING EXERCISE

Many of Jack London's stories share similar themes. Which of his stories has a theme that is most similar to In a Far Country? Write an essay comparing the themes of the two stories. Include at least two quotes from each story to support your stance.

LESSON TWELVE: IN A FAR COUNTRY

Story Summary _____ (possible 40 pts.)
Discussion Question _____ (possible 10 pts.)

Writing Exercise
    Originality and Creativity   _____ (possible 10 pts.)
    Overall Organization   _____ (possible 10 pts.)
    Language and Style   _____ (possible 10 pts.)
    Composition is neat   _____ (possible 10 pts.)
    Grammar and Spelling   _____ (possible 10 pts.)

                                                Total _____

NORTHLAND STORIES

LESSON 13: THE PRIESTLY PREROGATIVE

BEFORE YOU READ
Quote from the Reading
Look for this quote in your reading and pay special attention to its context:

"O what a fool I was to ever let you wag your silly tongue! Thank your God you are not a common man, for I'd – but the priestly prerogative must be exercised, eh? Well, you have exercised it."

VOCABULARY
Look for these words in your reading:

Indolent – disliking effort or activity
Belligerently – eager to or showing eagerness to fight
Scapegoat – a person or thing taking the blame for others

READING
Read: *The Priestly Prerogative* (Pages 150-162)

NOW THAT YOU'VE READ THE ASSIGNED STORY
Reread the quote above. Who said this quote? What do you think he meant by this quote?

_____
_____
_____
_____
_____
_____
_____
_____
_____
_____
_____
_____
_____
_____

STORY SUMMARY

Summarize *The Priestly Prerogative* below.

DISCUSSION

According to this story, how were women treated differently than men during the Klondike gold rush?

WRITING EXERCISE

Father Roubeau goes to great lengths to convince Grace to stay with her husband. Write a persuasive letter to one of the characters in the story to convince them of anything that you want. Include at least three points to support your position. You may include your own creative ideas in your letter.

LESSON THIRTEEN: THE PRIESTLY PERROGATIVE

Story Summary _____ (possible 40 pts.)
Discussion Question _____ (possible 10 pts.)

Writing Exercise
    Originality and Creativity   _____ (possible 10 pts.)
    Overall Organization   _____ (possible 10 pts.)
    Language and Style   _____ (possible 10 pts.)
    Composition is neat   _____ (possible 10 pts.)
    Grammar and Spelling   _____ (possible 10 pts.)

                      Total _____

NORTHLAND STORIES

LESSON 14: THE WIFE OF A KING

BEFORE YOU READ
Quote from the Reading
Look for this quote in your reading and pay special attention to its context:

"But somehow discontent fell upon him; he felt vague yearnings for his own kind, for the life he had been shut out from – a general sort of desire, which men sometimes feel, to break out and taste the prime of living."

VOCABULARY
Look for these words in your reading:

Obsolete – no longer useful
Renegade – an individual who rejects lawful or conventional behavior
Chivalry – an honorable or respectable way of behaving especially towards women

READING
Read: *The Wife of a King* (Pages 163-178)

NOW THAT YOU'VE READ THE ASSIGNED STORY
Reread the quote above. Who is this quote referring to? Rewrite the quote in your own words.

_____
_____
_____
_____
_____
_____
_____
_____
_____
_____
_____
_____
_____
_____

STORY SUMMARY

Summarize *The Wife of a King* below.

DISCUSSION

What do you think about the plan that Malemute Kid came up with for Madeline to imitate an English woman?

WRITING EXERCISE

Does *The Wife of the King* remind you of another story where the protagonist disguises his/her identity to accomplish a purpose? Compare Madeline to that character in a one-page essay. Describe what steps each character took to conceal his/her identity. Compare the outcomes and lessons learned in each story.

LESSON FOURTEEN: THE WIFE OF A KING

Story Summary _____ (possible 40 pts.)
Discussion Question _____ (possible 10 pts.)

Writing Exercise
    Originality and Creativity _____ (possible 10 pts.)
    Overall Organization _____ (possible 10 pts.)
    Language and Style _____ (possible 10 pts.)
    Composition is neat _____ (possible 10 pts.)
    Grammar and Spelling _____ (possible 10 pts.)

                        Total _____

NORTHLAND STORIES

LESSON 15: THE WISDOM OF THE TRAIL

BEFORE YOU READ
Quote from the Reading
Look for this quote in your reading and pay special attention to its context:

"A few words, my comrades, for your own good, that ye may yet perchance live. I shall give you the law; on his own head be the death of him that breaks it."

VOCABULARY
Look for these words in your reading:

Venerating – with regard to reverential respect or with admiring deference
Reluctant – showing doubt or unwillingness
Expedition – journey or trip undertaken for a specific purpose

READING
Read: *The Wisdom of the Trail* (Pages 179-186)

NOW THAT YOU'VE READ THE ASSIGNED STORY
Reread the quote above. Who said this quote? What "law" was he speaking about?

_____
_____
_____
_____
_____
_____
_____
_____
_____
_____
_____
_____
_____
_____
_____
_____

STORY SUMMARY

Summarize *The Wisdom of the Trail* below.

DISCUSSION

What do you think about the way Sitka Charley treated the men that he traveled with? Do you think that he could have done things differently? Explain your answer.

WRITING EXERCISE

Imagine that you are getting ready to go on a road trip with your family and a good friend. You want to prepare your friend for what he/she might encounter while traveling with your family. Explain any rules that your family members follow and ways that they tend to do things. Write out your instructions in the form of a letter, dialogue or short story.

LESSON FIFTEEN: THE WISDOM OF THE TRAIL

Story Summary _____ (possible 40 pts.)
Discussion Question _____ (possible 10 pts.)

Writing Exercise
    Originality and Creativity   _____ (possible 10 pts.)
    Overall Organization   _____ (possible 10 pts.)
    Language and Style   _____ (possible 10 pts.)
    Composition is neat   _____ (possible 10 pts.)
    Grammar and Spelling   _____ (possible 10 pts.)

                                   Total _____

NORTHLAND STORIES

LESSON 16: AN ODYSSEY OF THE NORTH

BEFORE YOU READ

Quote from the Reading

Look for this quote in your reading and pay special attention to its context:

"I will talk of the things which were, in my own way; but you will understand. I will begin at the beginning, and tell of myself and the woman, and, after that, of the man."

VOCABULARY

Look for these words in your reading:

Irrelevantly – not relevant or pertinent
Lore – a particular body of knowledge or tradition
Schooner – a ship with a fore-and-aft rig and two more masts

READING

Read: *An Odyssey of the North* (Pages 187-217)

NOW THAT YOU'VE READ THE ASSIGNED STORY

Reread the quote above. Who said this quote? Who are the woman and man that he is speaking about?

STORY SUMMARY

Summarize *An Odyssey of the North* below. What do you think is the theme of this story?

DISCUSSION

Why do you think Unga did not want to go back to Akatan with Naass?

WRITING EXERCISE

There are many ways to tell a story. In *The Odyssey of the North*, Jack London allows his character Naass to tell the backstory that explains who he is and what happened to him. Write your own short story employing the use of a backstory. Imitate Jack London by beginning your story with some unanswered questions, and then allow one of your characters to fill in the blanks with a backstory.

LESSON SIXTEEN: AN ODYSSEY OF THE NORTH

Story Summary _____ (possible 40 pts.)
Discussion Question _____ (possible 10 pts.)

Writing Exercise
    Originality and Creativity   _____ (possible 10 pts.)
    Overall Organization   _____ (possible 10 pts.)
    Language and Style   _____ (possible 10 pts.)
    Composition is neat   _____ (possible 10 pts.)
    Grammar and Spelling   _____ (possible 10 pts.)

                                                   Total _____

NORTHLAND STORIES

LESSON 17: TO BUILD A FIRE

BEFORE YOU READ

Quote from the Reading

Look for this quote in your reading and pay special attention to its context:

"Nevertheless he was aware of a thrill of joy, of exultation. He was doing something, achieving something, mastering the elements. Once he laughed aloud in sheer strength of life, and with his clenched fist defied the frost. He was its master."

VOCABULARY

Look for these words in your reading:

Precept – a command or principle intended especially as a general rule of action
Mishap – an unfortunate accident
Foresight – the act or power of foreseeing

READING

Read: *To Build a Fire* (Pages 218-225)

NOW THAT YOU'VE READ THE ASSIGNED STORY

Reread the quote above. What would you say to Tom Vincent about this quote after reading this story?

_____
_____
_____
_____
_____
_____
_____
_____
_____
_____
_____
_____
_____

STORY SUMMARY

Summarize *To Build a Fire* below. Why does the story start and end with the precept, "Never travel alone!"?

DISCUSSION

At the beginning of the story, that man is motivated to travel 30 miles to meet his friends. How did his motivation change throughout the story? Why?

WRITING EXERCISE

Write an alternate ending to the story. Will Tom encounter a stranger in his travels? Does his dog somehow help him? Will he survive in your story?

LESSON SEVENTEEN: TO BUILD A FIRE

Story Summary _____ (possible 40 pts.)
Discussion Question _____ (possible 10 pts.)

Writing Exercise
    Originality and Creativity   _____ (possible 10 pts.)
    Overall Organization   _____ (possible 10 pts.)
    Language and Style   _____ (possible 10 pts.)
    Composition is neat   _____ (possible 10 pts.)
    Grammar and Spelling   _____ (possible 10 pts.)

                              Total _____

JACK LONDON'S JOURNEY

LESSON 18: TOWARD FAME AND FORTUNE

READING

Read: *Toward Fame and Fortune* (Pages 226-272)

COMPREHENSION QUESTIONS

1) What was Jack London's birth name? Why was his name changed to Jack London? Where was he born?

2) Was Jack London's prospecting trip in 1897 successful? How did he finance the trip?

3) Name two of Jack London's strongest literary influences?

4) How did Jack London begin his writing career? What were some of the obstacles that he faced to becoming a writer?

DISCUSSION

Which Jack London story is your favorite and why?

A Thousand Deaths

In the story, *A Thousand Deaths*, who died a thousand deaths? Did the ending surprise you?

FINAL ESSAY

Write your final essay on one of the following topics:

1) How did the events in Jack London's life influence his writing? Give specific examples from the stories that you read and the facts that you learned about him in the biography lesson.

2) Write an essay describing three reoccurring themes that Jack London wrote about in his stories. Conclude with your opinion on why he often wrote about these particular themes.

3) As we learned in the biography lesson, Jack London did not have an easy road to become a famous writer. Write an essay about his journey to becoming a writer. How did he start writing? Did he have success right away? Describe his work ethic.

LESSON EIGHTEEN: TOWARD FAME AND FORTUNE

Discussion Question _____ (possible 10 pts.)
A Thousand Deaths _____ (possible 40 pts.)

Final Essay
    Originality and Creativity   _____ (possible 10 pts.)
    Overall Organization   _____ (possible 10 pts.)
    Language and Style   _____ (possible 10 pts.)
    Composition is neat   _____ (possible 10 pts.)
    Grammar and Spelling   _____ (possible 10 pts.)

                                                                        Total _____

Northland Vocabulary
Crossword Puzzle

Read the Across and Down clues and fill in the blank boxes that match the number on the clues

ACROSS
2   A person or thing taking the blame for others
4   A particular body of knowledge or tradition
6   A person or a thing out of place in time
8   Nearness in place or time
9   An unfortunate accident
11 Showing doubt or unwillingness
13 Disliking effort or activity
14 A surprising or irregular change
16 Relating to a primitive or early age
17 A ship with a fore-and-aft rig and two more masts
19 An act or instance of protest
21 Contradictory or opposed to common sense
22 Something different, abnormal or strange
23 Pity or sympathy
24 With regard to reverential respect or with admiring deference
25 Boring from being always the same
27 An honorable or respectable way of behaving especially towards women
28 An individual who rejects lawful or conventional behavior
29 Not relevant or pertinent
30 Showing kindly feelings or intentions

DOWN
1   A disease or disorder of the body or mind
3   Stubbornly or annoyingly persistent
5   Journey or trip undertaken for a specific purpose
7   No longer useful
10 Playful banter
12 Suited by nature, character or design to a particular use
15 A division of society based upon differences of wealth, rank, or occupation
18 Eager to or showing eagerness to fight
20 The act or power of foreseeing
26 A command or principle intended especially as a general rule of action

Northland Vocabulary
Crossword Puzzle

Read the Across and Down clues and fill in the blank boxes that match the number on the clues

119

Made in United States
Troutdale, OR
12/03/2024

25738675R00073